SOUND™ INNOVATIONS

ENSEMBLE DEVELOPMENT

Chorales and Warm-up Exercises for Tone, Technique and Rhythm

INTERMEDIATE CONCERT BAND

Peter **BOONSHAFT** | Chris **BERNOTAS**

Thank you for making *Sound Innovations: Ensemble Development* a part of your concert band curriculum. With 412 exercises, including over 70 chorales by some of today's most renowned composers for concert band, it is our hope you will find this book to be a valuable resource in helping you grow in your understanding and abilities as an ensemble musician.

An assortment of exercises are grouped by key and presented in a variety of intermediate difficulty levels. Where possible, several exercises in the same category are provided to allow for variety while accomplishing the goals of that specific type of exercise. You will notice that many exercises and chorales are clearly marked with dynamics, articulations, style, and tempo for you to practice those aspects of performance. Other exercises are intentionally left for you or your teacher to determine how best to use them in reaching your performance goals.

Whether you are progressing through exercises to better your technical facility or to challenge your musicianship with beautiful chorales, we are confident you will be excited, motivated, and inspired by using *Sound Innovations: Ensemble Development*.

Alfred

© 2012 Alfred Music Publishing Co., Inc.
Sound Innovations™ is a trademark of Alfred Music Publishing Co., Inc.
All Rights Reserved including Public Performance

ISBN-10: 0-7390-6769-9
ISBN-13: 978-0-7390-6769-7

Instrument photos courtesy of Yamaha Corporation of America Band & Orchestral Division

Concert B♭ Major (Your C Major)

1 PASSING THE TONIC

2 PASSING THE TONIC

3 PASSING THE TONIC

4 PASSING THE TONIC

5 PASSING THE TONIC

6 BREATHING AND LONG TONES

7 BREATHING AND LONG TONES

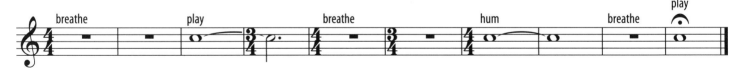

8 BREATHING AND LONG TONES

9 BREATHING AND LONG TONES

3

CONCERT B♭ MAJOR SCALE (YOUR C MAJOR SCALE)

SCALE PATTERN

SCALE PATTERN

SCALE PATTERN

SCALE PATTERN

SCALE PATTERN

CHANGING SCALE RHYTHM

CONCERT B♭ CHROMATIC SCALE (YOUR C CHROMATIC SCALE)

18 FLEXIBILITY

19 FLEXIBILITY

20 ARPEGGIOS

21 ARPEGGIOS

22 INTERVALS

23 INTERVALS

24 BALANCE AND INTONATION: PERFECT INTERVALS

25 BALANCE AND INTONATION: DIATONIC HARMONY

26 BALANCE AND INTONATION: FAMILY BALANCE

27 BALANCE AND INTONATION: LAYERED TUNING

28 BALANCE AND INTONATION: MOVING CHORD TONES

29 BALANCE AND INTONATION: SHIFTING CHORD QUALITIES

30 EXPANDING INTERVALS: DOWNWARD IN PARALLEL OCTAVES

31 EXPANDING INTERVALS: DOWNWARD IN PARALLEL FIFTHS

32 EXPANDING INTERVALS: DOWNWARD IN TRIADS

33 EXPANDING INTERVALS: UPWARD IN PARALLEL OCTAVES

34 EXPANDING INTERVALS: UPWARD IN TRIADS

35 RHYTHM

36 **RHYTHM**

37 **RHYTHM**

38 **RHYTHM**

39 **RHYTHM**

40 **RHYTHMIC SUBDIVISION**

41 **RHYTHMIC SUBDIVISION**

42 **RHYTHMIC SUBDIVISION**

43 **METER**

14 PHRASING

15 PHRASING

16 ARTICULATION

17 DYNAMICS

18 ETUDE

19 ETUDE

Concert G Minor (Your A Minor)

61 PASSING THE TONIC

62 BREATHING AND LONG TONES

63 CONCERT G NATURAL MINOR SCALE (YOUR A NATURAL MINOR SCALE)

64 CONCERT G HARMONIC AND MELODIC MINOR SCALES

65 SCALE PATTERN

66 CONCERT G CHROMATIC SCALE (YOUR A CHROMATIC SCALE)

67 FLEXIBILITY

68 FLEXIBILITY

69 ARPEGGIOS

70 ARPEGGIOS

71 INTERVALS

72 INTERVALS

73 BALANCE AND INTONATION: DIATONIC HARMONY

74 BALANCE AND INTONATION: MOVING CHORD TONES

75 BALANCE AND INTONATION: LAYERED TUNING

76 BALANCE AND INTONATION: FAMILY BALANCE

77 EXPANDING INTERVALS: DOWNWARD IN PARALLEL FIFTHS

78 EXPANDING INTERVALS: UPWARD IN PARALLEL THIRDS

79 **RHYTHM**

80 **RHYTHM**

81 **RHYTHM**

82 **RHYTHMIC SUBDIVISION**

83 **RHYTHMIC SUBDIVISION**

84 **ARTICULATION AND DYNAMICS**

85 **ETUDE**

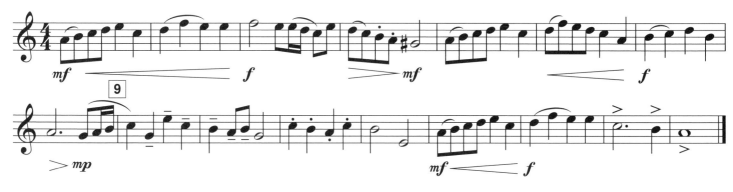

36 CHORALE

Larghetto

Robert Sheldon

37 CHORALE

Moderato

Michael Story (ASCAP)

38 CONCERT G MINOR SCALE & CHORALE

Chris M. Bernotas (ASCAP)

39 CHORALE

Moderately slow, smoothly

Andrew Boysen, Jr.

40 CHORALE

Sad and expressive, freely

Rossano Galante

Concert E♭ Major (Your F Major)

91 PASSING THE TONIC

92 PASSING THE TONIC

93 PASSING THE TONIC

94 PASSING THE TONIC

95 PASSING THE TONIC

96 BREATHING AND LONG TONES

97 BREATHING AND LONG TONES

98 BREATHING AND LONG TONES

99 BREATHING AND LONG TONES

15

00 CONCERT E♭ MAJOR SCALE (YOUR F MAJOR SCALE)

01 SCALE PATTERN

02 SCALE PATTERN

03 SCALE PATTERN

04 SCALE PATTERN

05 SCALE PATTERN

06 CHANGING SCALE RHYTHM

07 CONCERT E♭ CHROMATIC SCALE (YOUR F CHROMATIC SCALE)

108 **FLEXIBILITY**

109 **FLEXIBILITY**

110 **ARPEGGIOS**

111 **ARPEGGIOS**

112 **INTERVALS**

113 **INTERVALS**

114 **BALANCE AND INTONATION: PERFECT INTERVALS**

115 **BALANCE AND INTONATION: DIATONIC HARMONY**

116 **BALANCE AND INTONATION: FAMILY BALANCE**

17 **BALANCE AND INTONATION: LAYERED TUNING**

18 **BALANCE AND INTONATION: LAYERED TUNING**

19 **BALANCE AND INTONATION: SHIFTING CHORD QUALITIES**

20 **EXPANDING INTERVALS: DOWNWARD IN PARALLEL OCTAVES**

21 **EXPANDING INTERVALS: DOWNWARD IN PARALLEL FIFTHS**

22 **EXPANDING INTERVALS: DOWNWARD IN TRIADS**

23 **EXPANDING INTERVALS: UPWARD IN PARALLEL OCTAVES**

24 **EXPANDING INTERVALS: UPWARD IN TRIADS**

125 RHYTHM

126 RHYTHM

127 RHYTHM

128 RHYTHM

129 RHYTHM

130 RHYTHMIC SUBDIVISION

131 RHYTHMIC SUBDIVISION

132 RHYTHMIC SUBDIVISION

33 METER

34 PHRASING

35 PHRASING

36 ARTICULATION

37 DYNAMICS

38 ETUDE

39 ETUDE

20

140 CHORALE

Adagio, wistfully

Todd Stalter

141 CHORALE

Randall D. Standridge (ASCAP)

142 CONCERT E♭ MAJOR SCALE & CHORALE

Chris M. Bernotas (ASCAP)

143 CHORALE

Michael Story (ASCAP)

Moderato

144 CHORALE

Andrew Boysen, Jr.

Slow and delicate

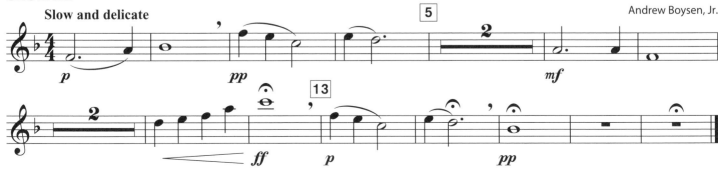

Concert C Minor (Your D Minor)

150 **PASSING THE TONIC**

151 **BREATHING AND LONG TONES**

152 **CONCERT C NATURAL MINOR SCALE (YOUR D NATURAL MINOR SCALE)**

153 **CONCERT C HARMONIC AND MELODIC MINOR SCALES**

154 **SCALE PATTERN**

155 **CONCERT C CHROMATIC SCALE (YOUR D CHROMATIC SCALE)**

156 **FLEXIBILITY**

157 **FLEXIBILITY**

58 ARPEGGIOS

59 ARPEGGIOS

60 INTERVALS

61 INTERVALS

62 BALANCE AND INTONATION: DIATONIC HARMONY

63 BALANCE AND INTONATION: MOVING CHORD TONES

64 BALANCE AND INTONATION: LAYERED TUNING

65 BALANCE AND INTONATION: FAMILY BALANCE

66 EXPANDING INTERVALS: DOWNWARD IN TRIADS

67 EXPANDING INTERVALS: UPWARD IN TRIADS

168 **RHYTHM**

169 **RHYTHM**

170 **RHYTHM**

171 **RHYTHMIC SUBDIVISION**

172 **RHYTHMIC SUBDIVISION**

173 **ARTICULATION AND DYNAMICS**

174 **ETUDE**

75 CHORALE

Randall D. Standridge (ASCAP)

76 CHORALE

Roland Barrett

177 CONCERT C MINOR SCALE & CHORALE

Chris M. Bernotas (ASCAP)

178 CHORALE: MEINES LEBENS LETZTE ZEIT

From the Gotha Psalter, 1726
Harmonized by J.S. Bach (1685–1750)
Arranged by Todd Stalter

Maestoso

179 CHORALE

Rossano Galante

Dark and moody

Concert F Major (Your G Major)

180 **PASSING THE TONIC**

181 **BREATHING AND LONG TONES**

182 **CONCERT F MAJOR SCALE (YOUR G MAJOR SCALE)**

183 **SCALE PATTERN**

184 **SCALE PATTERN**

185 **CONCERT F CHROMATIC SCALE (YOUR G CHROMATIC SCALE)**

186 **FLEXIBILITY**

187 **FLEXIBILITY**

188 ARPEGGIOS

189 ARPEGGIOS

190 INTERVALS

191 BALANCE AND INTONATION: DIATONIC HARMONY

192 BALANCE AND INTONATION: FAMILY BALANCE

193 BALANCE AND INTONATION: LAYERED TUNING

194 BALANCE AND INTONATION: MOVING CHORD TONES

195 BALANCE AND INTONATION: SHIFTING CHORD QUALITIES

196 EXPANDING INTERVALS: DOWNWARD IN PARALLEL FIFTHS

197 EXPANDING INTERVALS: UPWARD IN PARALLEL FIFTHS

198 **RHYTHM**

199 **RHYTHM**

200 **RHYTHM**

201 **RHYTHMIC SUBDIVISION**

202 **RHYTHMIC SUBDIVISION**

203 **ARTICULATION AND DYNAMICS**

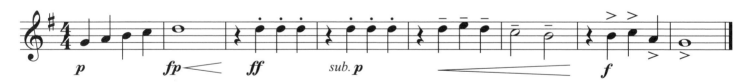

204 **ETUDE**

Concert D Minor (Your E Minor)

210 PASSING THE TONIC

211 BREATHING AND LONG TONES

212 CONCERT D NATURAL MINOR SCALE (YOUR E NATURAL MINOR SCALE)

213 CONCERT D HARMONIC AND MELODIC MINOR SCALES

214 SCALE PATTERN

215 SCALE PATTERN

216 CONCERT D CHROMATIC SCALE (YOUR E CHROMATIC SCALE)

217 FLEXIBILITY

218 FLEXIBILITY

219 ARPEGGIOS

220 ARPEGGIOS

221 INTERVALS

222 BALANCE AND INTONATION: DIATONIC HARMONY

223 BALANCE AND INTONATION: FAMILY BALANCE

224 BALANCE AND INTONATION: LAYERED TUNING

225 BALANCE AND INTONATON: MOVING CHORD TONES

226 EXPANDING INTERVALS: DOWNWARD IN TRIADS

227 EXPANDING INTERVALS: UPWARD IN TRIADS

228 RHYTHM

229 RHYTHM

230 RHYTHM

231 RHYTHMIC SUBDIVISION

232 RHYTHMIC SUBDIVISION

233 ARTICULATION AND DYNAMICS

234 ETUDE

Lyrical

Concert A♭ Major (Your B♭ Major)

240 PASSING THE TONIC

241 BREATHING AND LONG TONES

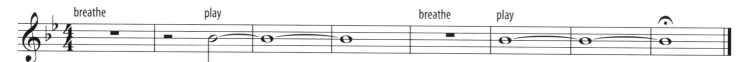

242 CONCERT A♭ MAJOR SCALE (YOUR B♭ MAJOR SCALE)

243 SCALE PATTERN

244 SCALE PATTERN

245 CONCERT A♭ CHROMATIC SCALE (YOUR B♭ CHROMATIC SCALE)

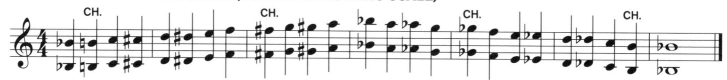

246 FLEXIBILITY

247 FLEXIBILITY

248 **ARPEGGIOS**

249 **ARPEGGIOS**

L (upper) L (upper)

250 **INTERVALS**

251 **BALANCE AND INTONATION: DIATONIC HARMONY**

252 **BALANCE AND INTONATION: FAMILY BALANCE**

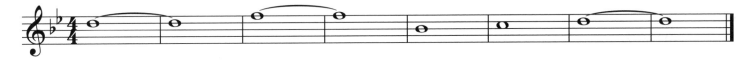

253 **BALANCE AND INTONATION: LAYERED TUNING**

254 **BALANCE AND INTONATION: MOVING CHORD TONES**

255 **EXPANDING INTERVALS: DOWNWARD IN PARALLEL FIFTHS**

256 **EXPANDING INTERVALS: UPWARD IN PARALLEL THIRDS**

Concert F Minor (Your G Minor)

270 PASSING THE TONIC

271 BREATHING AND LONG TONES

272 CONCERT F NATURAL MINOR SCALE (YOUR G NATURAL MINOR SCALE)

273 CONCERT F HARMONIC AND MELODIC MINOR SCALES

274 SCALE PATTERN

275 CONCERT F CHROMATIC SCALE (YOUR G CHROMATIC SCALE)

276 FLEXIBILITY

277 FLEXIBILITY

278 ARPEGGIOS

279 **ARPEGGIOS**

280 **INTERVALS**

281 **INTERVALS**

282 **BALANCE AND INTONATION: DIATONIC HARMONY**

283 **BALANCE AND INTONATION: FAMILY BALANCE**

284 **BALANCE AND INTONATION: LAYERED TUNING**

285 **BALANCE AND INTONATION: MOVING CHORD TONES**

286 **EXPANDING INTERVALS: DOWNWARD IN TRIADS**

287 **EXPANDING INTERVALS: UPWARD IN TRIADS**

288 **RHYTHM**

289 **RHYTHM**

290 **RHYTHM**

291 **RHYTHMIC SUBDIVISION**

292 **RHYTHMIC SUBDIVISION**

293 **ARTICULATION AND DYNAMICS**

294 **ETUDE**

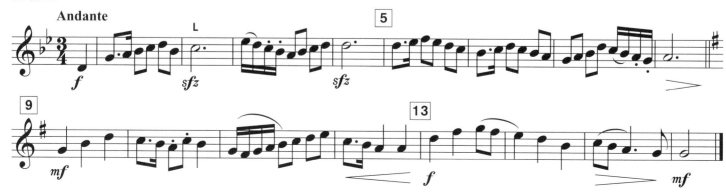

295 CHORALE

Randall D. Standridge (ASCAP)

296 CHORALE

Roland Barrett

297 CONCERT F MINOR SCALE & CHORALE

Chris M. Bernotas (ASCAP)

A

B

298 CHORALE

Robert Sheldon

Andante

299 CHORALE

Ralph Ford (ASCAP)

Lament

Concert D♭ Major (Your E♭ Major)

300 BREATHING AND LONG TONES

301 CONCERT D♭ MAJOR SCALE (YOUR E♭ MAJOR SCALE)

302 SCALE PATTERN

303 SCALE PATTERN

304 SCALE PATTERN

305 FLEXIBILITY

306 ARPEGGIOS

307 INTERVALS

08 BALANCE AND INTONATION: FAMILY BALANCE

09 BALANCE AND INTONATION: LAYERED TUNING

10 EXPANDING INTERVALS: DOWNWARD AND UPWARD IN PARALLEL OCTAVES

11 ARTICULATION AND DYNAMICS

12 ETUDE

13 ETUDE

14 CHORALE

Andrew Boysen, Jr.

15 CHORALE

Todd Stalter

Concert B♭ Minor (Your C Minor)

316 BREATHING AND LONG TONES

317 CONCERT B♭ NATURAL MINOR SCALE (YOUR C NATURAL MINOR SCALE)

318 CONCERT B♭ HARMONIC AND MELODIC MINOR SCALES

319 SCALE PATTERN

320 SCALE PATTERN

321 FLEXIBILITY

322 ARPEGGIOS

323 INTERVALS

324 BALANCE AND INTONATION: LAYERED TUNING

25 **BALANCE AND INTONATION: MOVING CHORD TONES**

26 **EXPANDING INTERVALS: DOWNWARD IN TRIADS**

27 **ARTICULATION AND DYNAMICS**

28 **ETUDE**

Slowly

29 **ETUDE**

Dramatically

30 **CHORALE**

Michael Story (ASCAP)

Moderately slow

31 **CHORALE**

Robert Sheldon

Andante

Concert C Major (Your D Major)

332 **BREATHING AND LONG TONES**

333 **CONCERT C MAJOR SCALE (YOUR D MAJOR SCALE)**

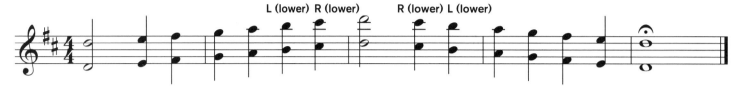

334 **SCALE PATTERN**

335 **SCALE PATTERN**

336 **FLEXIBILITY**

337 **ARPEGGIOS**

338 **INTERVALS**

339 **INTERVALS**

340 **BALANCE AND INTONATION: FAMILY BALANCE**

41 BALANCE AND INTONATION: LAYERED TUNING

42 EXPANDING INTERVALS: DOWNWARD IN PARALLEL FIFTHS

43 ARTICULATION AND DYNAMICS

44 ETUDE

45 ETUDE

46 CHORALE

Ralph Ford (ASCAP)

47 CHORALE: LARGO FROM THE "NEW WORLD SYMPHONY"

Antonín Dvořák
Arranged by Michael Story (ASCAP)

Concert A Minor (Your B Minor)

348 BREATHING AND LONG TONES

349 CONCERT A NATURAL MINOR SCALE (YOUR B NATURAL MINOR SCALE)

350 CONCERT A HARMONIC AND MELODIC MINOR SCALES

351 SCALE PATTERN

352 FLEXIBILITY

353 ARPEGGIOS

354 INTERVALS

355 INTERVALS

356 BALANCE AND INTONATION: DIATONIC HARMONY

57 BALANCE AND INTONATION: FAMILY BALANCE

58 EXPANDING INTERVALS: DOWNWARD IN TRIADS

59 ARTICULATION AND DYNAMICS

60 ETUDE

61 ETUDE

62 CHORALE

Todd Stalter

63 CHORALE

Roland Barrett

Concert G Major (Your A Major)

364 **CONCERT G MAJOR SCALE (YOUR A MAJOR SCALE)**

365 **BALANCE AND INTONATION: FAMILY BALANCE**

366 **ETUDE**

367 **CHORALE**

Michael Story (ASCAP)

Concert E Minor (Your F# Minor)

368 **CONCERT E NATURAL MINOR SCALE (YOUR F# NATURAL MINOR SCALE)**

369 **CONCERT E HARMONIC AND MELODIC MINOR SCALES**

370 **BALANCE AND INTONATION: LAYERED TUNING**

371 **ETUDE**

372 **CHORALE**

Chris M. Bernotas (ASCAP)

Advancing Rhythm and Meter

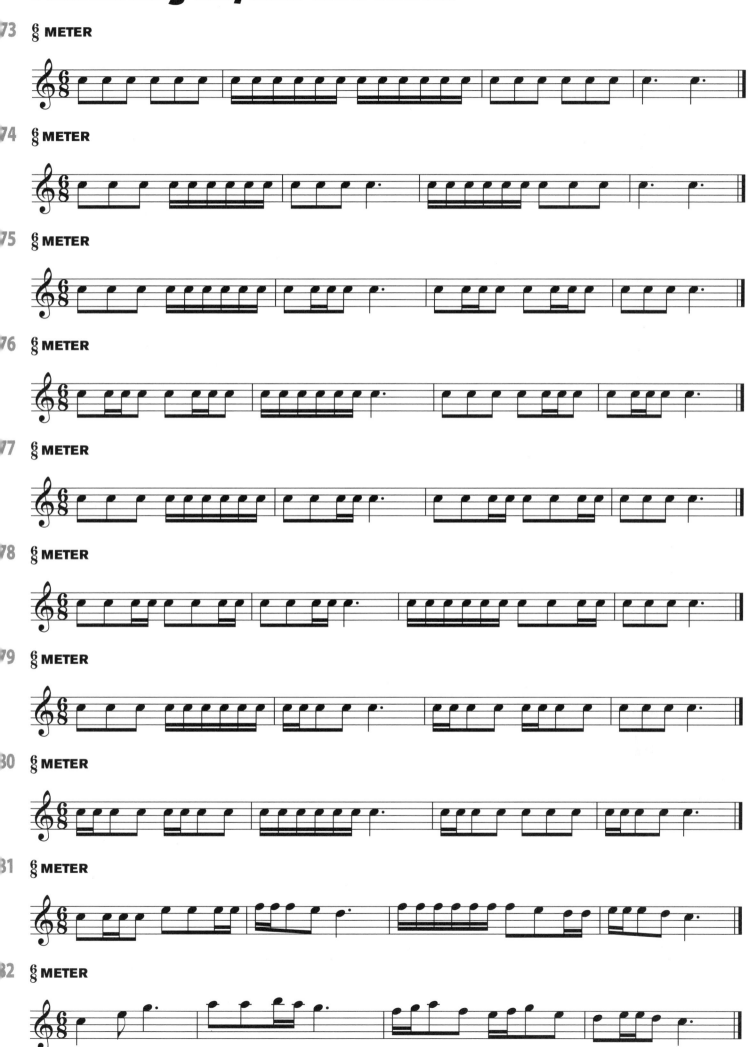

383 §8 METER

384 §8 METER

385 §8 METER

386 §8 METER

387 §8 METER

388 §8 METER

389 §8 METER

390 §8 METER

391 **CHANGING METERS: 4/4 AND 6/8**

392 **CHANGING METERS: 3/4 AND 6/8**

93 TRIPLETS

94 TRIPLETS

95 TRIPLETS

96 TRIPLETS

97 TRIPLETS

98 TRIPLETS

99 TRIPLETS

00 TRIPLETS

01 TRIPLETS

02 TRIPLETS

403 $\frac{3}{8}$ **METER**

404 $\frac{3}{8}$ **METER**

405 $\frac{9}{8}$ **METER**

406 $\frac{9}{8}$ **METER**

407 $\frac{12}{8}$ **METER**

408 $\frac{12}{8}$ **METER**

409 $\frac{5}{8}$ **METER**

(2+3)   (3+2)

410 $\frac{5}{8}$ **METER**

(2+3)   (3+2)

411 $\frac{7}{8}$ **METER**

(2+2+3)

412 $\frac{7}{8}$ **METER**

(2+2+3)

Clarinet Fingering Chart

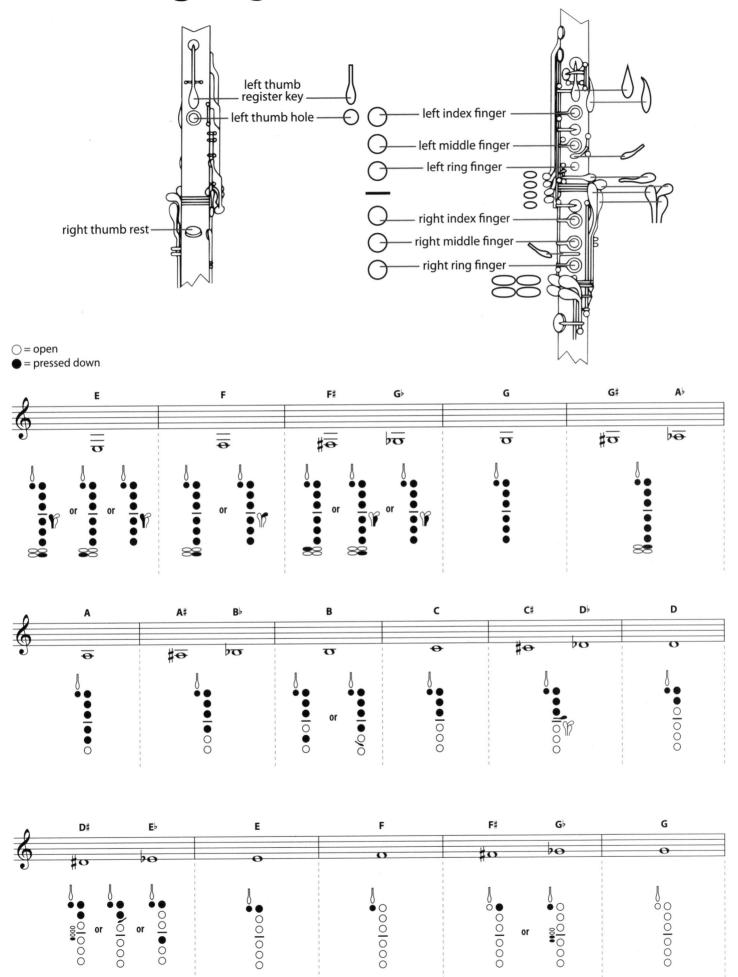

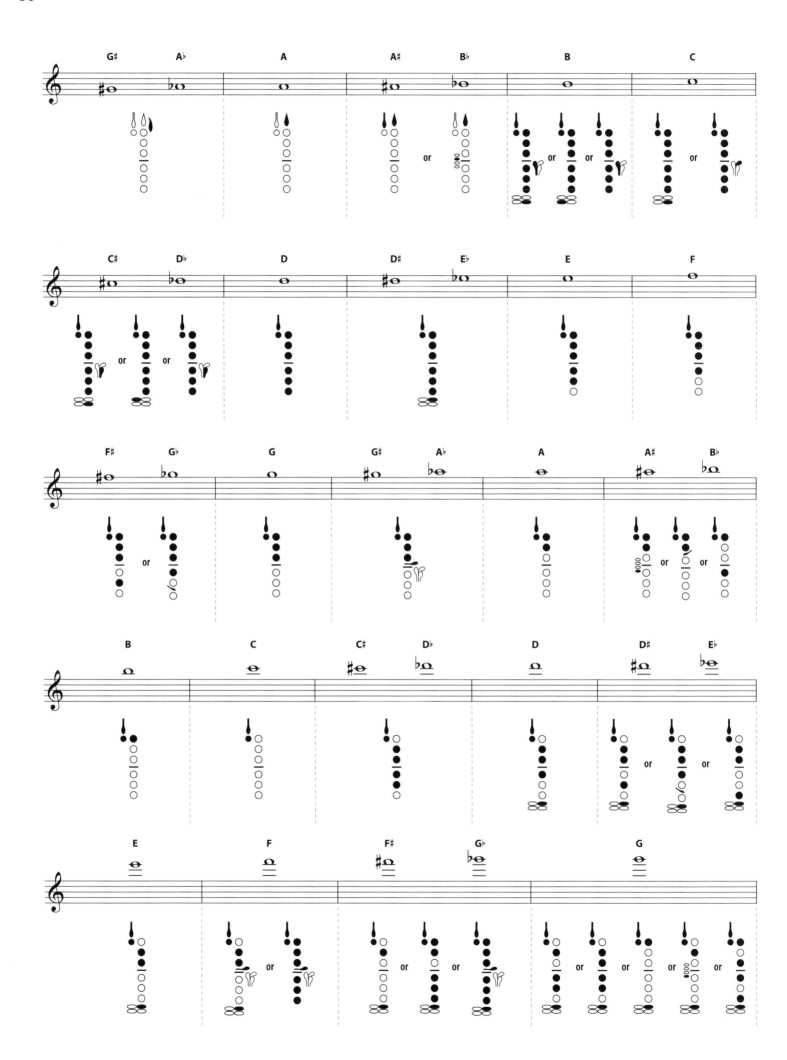